HAL•LEONARD®

VIOLIN PLAY-ALONG

AUDIO ACCESS INCLUDED

PLAYBACK+
Speed • Pitch • Balance • Loop

THE PIANO GUYS
WONDERS

D0613709

To access audio visit:
www.halleonard.com/mylibrary

Enter Code
6492-6398-7260-7043

ISBN 978-1-4950-4765-7

HAL•LEONARD®
CORPORATION

7777 W. BLUEMOUND RD. P.O. BOX 13819 MILWAUKEE, WI 53213

Visit Hal Leonard Online at
www.halleonard.com

Audio Arrangements by The Piano Guys

Visit The Piano Guys at:
thepianoguys.com

CONTENTS

As performed by The Piano Guys

Story of My Life

**Words and Music by Jamie Scott, John Henry Ryan, Julian Bunetta,
Harry Styles, Liam Payne, Louis Tomlinson, Niall Horan and Zain Malik
Arranged by Steven Sharp Nelson and Al van der Beek**

As performed by The Piano Guys

Let It Go

from Disney's Animated Feature FROZEN

Music and Lyrics by Kristen Anderson-Lopez and Robert Lopez
Arranged by Al van der Beek, Jon Schmidt and Steven Sharp Nelson
Inspired by Concerto No. 4 in F Minor, Op. 8, RV297, "Winter" by Antonio Vivaldi

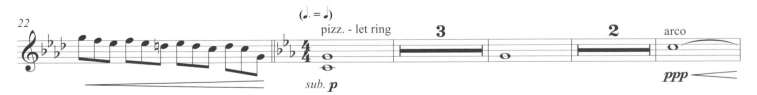

rit.

9

As performed by The Piano Guys

Ants Marching/Ode to Joy

Words and Music by David J. Matthews
Arranged by Al van der Beek, Jon Schmidt and Steven Sharp Nelson
Inspired by the "Ode to Joy" melody from
Symphony No. 9 in D Minor, Op. 125 by Ludwig van Beethoven

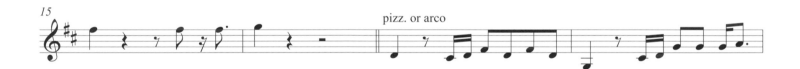

Father's Eyes

By Al van der Beek and Steven Sharp Nelson

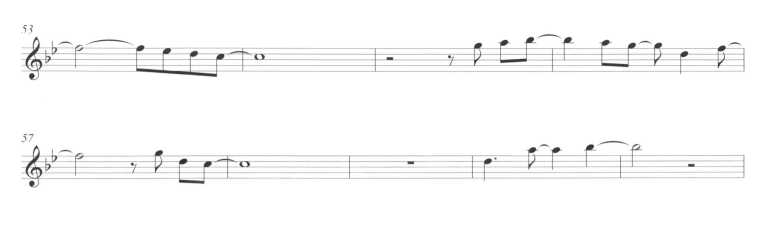

As performed by The Piano Guys

Kung Fu Piano: Cello Ascends

"Oogway Ascends"
By Hans Zimmer, John Powell and Henry Jackman
Arranged by Al van der Beek, Jon Schmidt and Steven Sharp Nelson
Based upon and inspired by Frederick Chopin's Prelude Op. 28 No. 20 in C minor

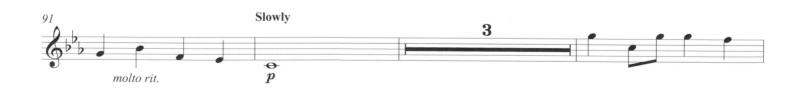

As performed by The Piano Guys

The Mission/How Great Thou Art

THE MISSION
from the Motion Picture THE MISSION
Music by Ennio Morricone
Arranged by Jon Schmidt,
Al van der Beek and Steven Sharp Nelson

HOW GREAT THOU ART
Words by Stuart K. Hine
Swedish Folk Melody Adapted and Arranged by
Stuart K. Hine
Arranged by Jon Schmidt,
Al van der Beek and Steven Sharp Nelson

As performed by The Piano Guys

Summer Jam

By Jon Schmidt and Steven Sharp Nelson

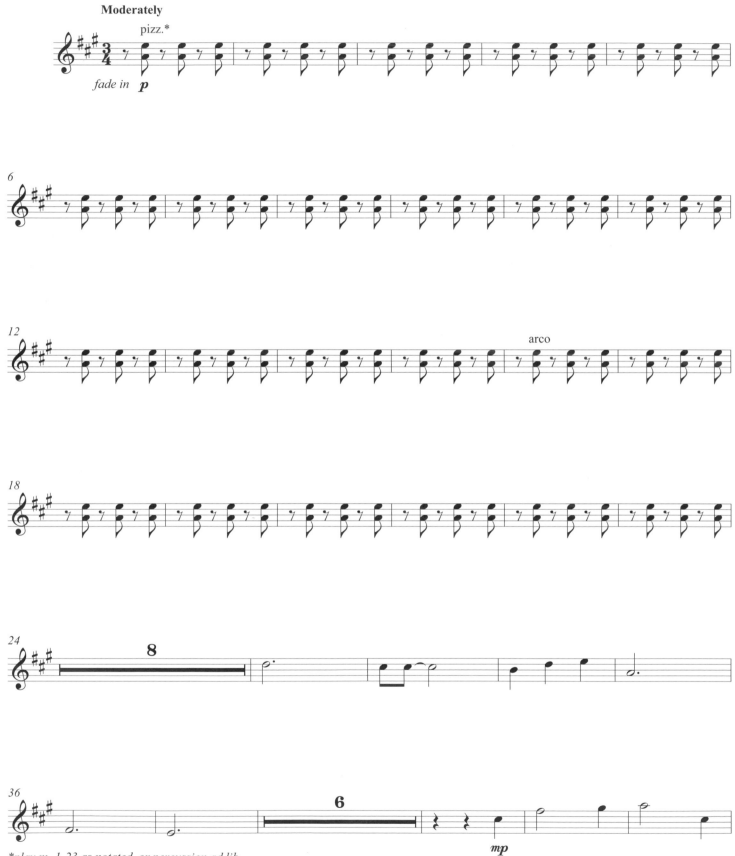

*play m. 1-23 as notated, or percussion ad lib.

Batman Evolution

Arranged by Al van der Beek and Steven Sharp Nelson

BATMAN THEME
By DANNY ELFMAN

BATMAN THEME
Words and Music by
NEAL HEFTI

LIKE A DOG CHASING CARS
Composed by HANS ZIMMER
and JAMES NEWTON HOWARD

As performed by The Piano Guys

Don't You Worry Child

Words and Music by Steve Angello, Axel Hedfors, Sebastian Ingrosso, Michel Zitron and Martin Lindstrom
Arranged by Arranged by Al van der Beek, Steven Sharp Nelson, Jon Schmidt and Shweta Subram

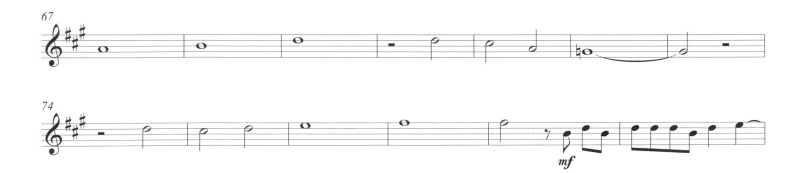

Home

Words and Music by Greg Holden and Drew Pearson
Arranged by Al van der Beek, Jon Schmidt and Steven Sharp Nelson
Inspired by "Going Home," *Largo* melody from Dvořák's *New World Symphony*

Pictures at an Exhibition

By Modest Mussorgsky
Arranged by Al van der Beek and Steven Sharp Nelson

Because of You

By Al van der Beek and Steven Sharp Nelson